FAERIES HITHER!

Faeries Hither! was first published in 1935 and now S. E. Archer's charming evocations of the Faery world are available again, with new illustrations by the gifted artist Brigid Murray.

The author's daughter Patricia H. Smyth has provided an illustrated biography of her mother to complete this tribute to a 'most gentle, unassuming and thoroughly good lady'.

FAERIES HITHER!

POEMS

by
S. E. Archer

with illustrations by
Brigid Murray

To Clive & Pip
with best wishes
Brigid Murray.
19/06/08

ARTHUR H. STOCKWELL LTD
Torrs Park   Ilfracombe   Devon
Established 1898
www.ahstockwell.co.uk

British Library Cataloguing-in-Publication Data.
A catalogue record for this book is available
from the British Library.

ISBN 978-0-7223-3885-8
Printed in Great Britain by
Arthur H. Stockwell Ltd
Torrs Park   Ilfracombe
Devon

Contents

Sheelagh Archer, 1916–2006

(A Biography by Patricia H. Smyth)

Sheelagh Elizabeth Anna Archer was born in Dublin on the 10th January 1916, the eldest daughter of Frederick Thomas Archer and Henrietta (née Walker). She had a younger sister, Joan, and a brother, Sean. Her father's family were from Dublin and her mother's from Carnew, County Wicklow.

Sheelagh's father was Catholic, and her mother, Protestant, Church of Ireland: mixed marriage was then a much more sensitive subject. Before the Easter Rising of 1916, and the subsequent civil war, the Protestant minority had much more political and social prestige. After 1921 the Protestant minority was conspicuous by its silence. The minority were mainly Unionist in politics and Protestant in religion. After the civil war they would never again enjoy the privileged position or power or social status hitherto enjoyed. The southern Unionists were mainly concentrated in South County Dublin, and parts of Cork. But not all members of the minority were characterised by loyalty to the British Crown. Henrietta Archer was ardently nationalistic, and she espoused her loyalty in many ways. Her children all bore Irish names.

Sheelagh's mother, Henrietta Archer.

Frederick worked as secretary to the prosperous firm of Baker and Wardell, tea and sugar merchants of 76 Thomas Street, Dublin, in the heart of the Liberties. The Archer family lived in a house owned by Frederick's mother on the Rathgar Road. In an early photograph we see a young nursemaid, Emily Thompson, in the back garden of the house in Rathgar, with Sheelagh, aged about six, standing on an elegant balloon-backed chair, holding a doll. She appears a determined and self-possessed little girl.

During the civil war many of the minority left their homes and went abroad because of insecurity of life and property. In 1922 the Archer children, accompanied by their mother and Essie Nolan, were sent from 'violent Dublin' to live in Achill Island for two years. The house where they lived was loaned to them by their family doctor, Dr Kathleen Lynn, who was also a close family friend. Dr Lynn served as a captain with the Irish Citizen Army during the 1916 Easter Rising. She herself had been imprisoned in Dublin Castle for her part in the Easter Rising.

Later she was employed in England as a doctor, due to lack of medical staff during the First World War. Interestingly, Sheelagh's mother appears in an early photograph wearing on her blouse a Tara brooch, which emblem was adopted as that of Inghinidhe na hÉireann, which was founded by Maud Gonne in 1900. It was to become one of the more enterprising and successful organisations of the growing independence movement in Ireland. It was a forerunner of Cumann na mBan – the female branch of the nationalist movement founded in 1914.

There is no doubt that during these early years the wild and remote environs of Achill impressed themselves on the mind and childish imagination of Sheelagh. Sheelagh was six when she came to live in Achill and eight when she left; and it was there that she developed a great love of nature and especially wild flowers. In later life she

*Joan held by her young nursemaid, Emily Thompson,
with Sheelagh standing on a chair in the back garden
of the house in Rathgar.*

Sheelagh as a baby with her parents Frederick and Henrietta Archer.

*Essie Nolan and the Archer children outside the house on
Achill Island (lent by Dr Kathleen Lynn).
Sheelagh is looking to her left and wearing her 'crown'.*

imparted her knowledge of natural history to her own three daughters. She also would have listened to the rich variety of storytelling on Achill Island, where Faeries were a very much accepted and revered part of Irish folklore. It is also certain that she acquired and retained a deep interest all her life in things of a supernatural nature. Sheelagh was very close to her mother, and she was greatly influenced by her. According to Sheelagh's sister Joan, "Mother was a beautiful and gracious lady, and had a nature to match: kind and generous, ambitious only for others, not for herself."

Essie Nolan, who came from County Wicklow, helped their mother to care for the children. A photograph which survives from this time shows Sheelagh holding a kitten, and wearing her 'crown'. Her sister Joan and flaxen-haired Sean also appear. On her marriage, Essie Nolan came to Henrietta Archer from her husband's mother – 'a family retainer'. Essie was very kind to the Archer children, and when she retired to her cottage at Poulaphouca the children visited her regularly. The area was later to become a reservoir and her cottage and others were demolished and then flooded.

Her sister Joan said that, as a young girl, Sheelagh was always 'the boss' and she did not suffer fools gladly. She was gentle but tenacious and always expected the best of everyone. She grew up a beautiful young lady with natural wavy brown hair. She had eyes of the most lovely shade of china blue. Her eyes, even up to her ninetieth year, kept their almost childlike quality of expression and youth.

While on Achill Island, Sheelagh was sent to be educated at a local convent; Joan remembers being taught the Lord's Prayer in Irish.

When the Archers eventually returned to Dublin they went to live for two years at Tichnoch, at the foot of the Dublin Mountains. After that, they moved again, to live

Essie Nolan with Joan (left), Sean and Sheelagh on Achill Island. Sheelagh is sporting her 'crown' and holding a kitten.

in a house on the summit of the Hill of Howth, courtesy again of Dr Kathleen Lynn. The two sisters were sent as boarders to be educated at the St Mary's, Anglican Convent, Clyde Road, Dublin. Sheelagh's father had since taken work as a sales rep for a bottling and glass company from Belgium. He visited hotels to get orders for various types of glassware. Henrietta Archer sent her two daughters for art classes to Evie Hone, the great stained-glass artist. While they attended, Mainie Jellet, one of Ireland's greatest female artists, often called to see Evie Hone. Sheelagh described Evie as a chatty little person, in whose home in Rathfarnham there was often the smell of home-baking. In contrast to Evie, Mainie Jellet was 'very silent and very nice woman'. Sheelagh maintained a deep interest in art and was a regular visitor to art galleries. From early photographs we can deduce that she was a keen athlete; as children we remember her doing cartwheels around the back garden in Clontarf, in her thirties.

Joan said that her elder sister was always clever, hard-working and conscientious. Sheelagh showed evidence of this academic ability when she won a scholarship into Alexandra College in 1933. Alexandra College was founded in 1866 for the education of young ladies some of whom aspired to become teachers. It was to become one of the foremost educational establishments of its time, and its reputation for academic excellence has been upheld to this day.

Sheelagh entered the Froebel department, where she was taught by Anne Casserley, amongst others. Miss Casserley was a teacher, author and artist of several children's books, including *The Whins on Knockattan* and other books of Donegal fairy tales. She remained friends with both Anne and Dora Casserley, who wrote a children's *History of Ireland*. They were kindly and quaint sisters, whose father was a Church of Ireland rector from Donegal. As a child I

Sheelagh Ledbetter (née Archer), 1916–2006.
Photo taken in 1939 on her engagement to John E. Ledbetter.

remember visiting the Casserleys in Glasnevin. Anne Casserley, dressed in grey knitted garments and thick grey hose, with a green eyeshade worn on her head, proceeded to go down on all fours and bark at us – "Wuf! Wuf! Wuf!" – to keep us amused. She must have been in her seventies at the time. Her sister was like a chirpy little bird with bright eyes and a throaty infectious laugh. Their joyous and self-effacing characters disguised two most scholarly and intelligent sisters. Sheelagh spent one year training as a primary-school teacher. Another contemporary student was Moira Cooke who became a teacher in Alexandra School. I was taught by her for several years, quite oblivious to the fact that my mother had also trained with her. In 1934 Sheelagh was offered a teaching post in Preston School, Navan, County Meath. Preston School originally stood on what is now the site of the large shopping centre in Navan. She eventually left to take up teaching in Bertrand and Rutland School, Eccles Street, Dublin. Both schools are long since gone.

All her life, Sheelagh loved poetry, and even into old age she could quote long passages of poems learnt in her earlier years. She greatly admired Walter de la Mare's poetry: she told us daughters that she corresponded with Walter de la Mare. She learnt to appreciate the romance of poetry from his work and admired the world of phantasy that he created, and his musical verse. I remember coming across some of his letters when, as a child of ten, I was looking through a dressing table. He wrote critiques of her work and encouraged her literary endeavours in his letters. Unfortunately, the only surviving evidence of correspondence between her and Walter de la Mare is a hand-written telegram, dated 10th January 1935, wishing Sheelagh 'Very many happy returns of the day' and signed by Walter de la Mare. In 1956 Walter de la Mare invited the family to afternoon tea while we were visiting London. As children who knew his poems 'Silver' and 'The

Birthday telegram from Walter de la Mare to Sheelagh on her 19th birthday — the year her poems (Faeries Hither!) were published.

The shop at 21 Essex Quay. John's father (right) with shop manager.

A grandfather clock, made by J. E. Ledbetter, clock and watchmakers.

John and Sheelagh on their engagement.

Listeners' we were greatly excited at the prospect of meeting him. Unfortunately Walter de la Mare took ill suddenly and our visit was cancelled. He died a few weeks later.

Whilst she was a teacher, Sheelagh belonged to a rambling club – she liked to relax by going for long walks in the mountains and countryside during her spare time. It was on one of these walks that she met a Mr Albert Ledbetter. He was blind as a result of a car accident. Through Albert – or Bertie, as he was usually known – Sheelagh met her future husband, John Edmund Ledbetter. She had heard that the house that the Ledbetters lived in – 23 Essex Quay – was well known to be haunted. She was curious to see the premises and called with a broken silver teapot to have it repaired. She said that her future husband came out from the back of the shop – "a very thin, dark curly-haired young man, with a jacket with sleeves far too short and a smile from ear to ear". John had had to leave school at the age of thirteen, and forgo his hopes of a medical career. His father died at the early age of fifty-seven, leaving his son to fend for the family. He worked in his late father's firm – a jeweller's and watchmaker's at Essex Quay, Dublin. Originally the Ledbetters had a shop at 93a Thomas Street, in the Dublin Liberties. They made watches and produced grandfather clocks. To this day one of the family clocks is retained in family ownership, in full working order. The Ledbetter firm moved first to 11 Essex Quay, then to 21 Essex Quay, and finally to 23 Essex Quay. In later years my father moved the business to 17 and 18 Nassau Street. Incidentally, when Temple Properties demolished 23 Essex Quay, under the foundations were found the ramparts of Isolde's Tower, with a row of six human skulls arranged along the base – people who had been beheaded in medieval times. Perhaps this is the source of the ghostly occurrences for which No. 23 was notorious.

Susan (Sheelagh's eldest daughter).

Patricia (Sheelagh's middle daughter).

Margaret (Sheelagh's youngest daughter).

Sheelagh and John married on 5th June 1940. Theirs was to be a most happy marriage. They had three daughters – Susan, Patricia and Margaret. Sheelagh gave up teaching and worked alongside her husband in the shop. Many of their customers became personal friends of the Ledbetters. John Ledbetter eventually bought out his mother's business and it grew and prospered under his direction. It eventually closed in 1984 as a result of a robbery at 17 and 18 Nassau Street. (A printer, William McGee, once carried out his work at 18 Nassau Street.) John E. Ledbetter was one of Dublin's oldest firms, having been founded in 1830 – older even than the famous Bewley's (1840). The Ledbetter ancestors came as French Huguenot refugees to Ireland in the seventeenth century. There is mention of Ledbetters in the vestry records of the Parish of St John the Evangelist, Dublin as far back as 1622.

John Ledbetter was a most respected antique-silver dealer and jeweller, and he was appointed Master of the Corporation of Goldsmiths of Ireland in 1951. He was extremely hard-working, genial and modest; and Sheelagh learned everything about silver and jewellery from her husband. He spent long hours at night auctions as a young teenager and gradually built up the business. He read a lot and learnt much of the trade from books and from talking to other members of the trade. He died at the age of sixty-three in 1973. Sheelagh continued the business along with her eldest daughter, Susan, until the robbery finished the trading there. She then left for London along with Susan and her husband. Sheelagh worked in London alongside Susan in a modest antique-silver business. She travelled into London every day, despite her failing health and vigour, until the age of eighty-four. She lived in Walthamstow until her death at the age of ninety.

She travelled with her daughter and her husband the length and breadth of England, exploring cities, museums and art galleries. She maintained her interest in the arts until the very end. During those years of failing health, Susan cared for and looked after her with love and attentiveness that was superhuman in its endeavour. She died on the 4th March 2006 at Whipps Cross Hospital, London, after a short illness. To the end she maintained her own special grace and dignity; and to this day she is deeply and sorely missed.

It was on the return journey from Sheelagh's funeral at Mount Jerome Cemetery that Joan, her eighty-nine-year-old sister, announced that Sheelagh once had a book published. Our mother had never told any of us daughters and it came as a complete shock and surprise to all. After some detective work, I discovered a copy of the little book of poetry in Trinity College Library Dublin.

It was during 1935 that Sheelagh had, as far as is known, her only book of poetry published. The book is *Faeries Hither!* by S. E. Archer, published by Arthur H. Stockwell, of Ludgate Hill, London. Stockwell's premises were bombed during the war and no copy or record of the little publication survives in their archives or that of their printers at Rushden. It is a very slight publication of only eight poems, but there is a quality and originality about the poems that is unique. The only available copies of these poems are in the copyright libraries of the Bodleian Library, Oxford; the British Library, London; and Trinity College Library Dublin. It is surmised that the poems were privately published and that her father, Frederick Thomas Archer, possibly paid for their publication. Joan also maintained that her father had a book of ghost stories published, but no record has been found to date.

The poems are most beautifully and dramatically illustrated by the gifted artist Brigid Murray, who is also the author of the outstanding novel *Figures in a Landscape*. Brigid has interpreted the poems as a dream sequence, and the originality and vividness of the illustrations add greatly to the richness of the work. They are wed wonderfully to the words of the poems and are unique. There is an awareness that we stand on the borders between two worlds – the world that we know and that of the supernatural.

This is how this book has come to be republished as a tribute to this most gentle, unassuming and thoroughly good lady. She imparted to her children the best lessons that life can teach – kindness, a deep and abiding love of all that is good, an appreciation of nature, the importance of hard work, and a gentle sense of humour. She has conveyed the sense of a Faery world that is everywhere about us if only we have the eyes to see.

The Faeries

I once met the Faeries
A long time ago,
Away in the country,
On mountains I know.

They just stood there, staring,
Then whispered very low,
With laughter the weirdest
I've heard of or know.

Their long hair was tangled,
Their eyes dusky blue,
Their forms brown and lanky –
For the rest, just like you.

Since then I've ne'er seen them,
Yet oft I know they're near;
They cause a sight sometimes,
And sometimes a tear.

A Faery Is Just Like a Toadstool

A Faery is just like a toadstool,
    Tiny lean and brown,
    You can never tell its age;
It comes out when the sun goes down.

A Faery's House

A little white house sprang up one night,
The rooms were pink, the roof was white;
But the house was magic, and – do you know? –
Before noon came it commenced to grow!
When seen next day, you'd scarce know it at all,
For the roof was brown, and the house was tall.
It was owned by Faeries, but 'twas far too small,
So they made it bigger to hold them all.

Faery Possessions

The scent of the lilac and taste of dew
Are what the garden Faeries brew.
The trees' green leaves and wild nuts sweet
Are what wood Faeries like to eat.
The dog-rose petals and clover red
Both make a meadow Faery's bed.
The bulrush flower and the marsh marigold
Are water Faeries' money, we're told.
The honied heather and the yellow whins
Are the mountain Faeries' homely inns.
The wild bog cotton and the burnet rose
Make the Faeries' brown, of their clothes.
The red-berried rowan and the lone hawthorn
Were Faery dwellings ere man was born.

The Faery Coach

If you wait, late in the evening,
Behind the prickle hedge,
Bounding the rough white road,
You may hear the Faery coach pass,
Carrying its Faery load.
You cannot see the horses,
But you will hear their feet,
Trotting along the highway –
Beat-beat, beat-beat, beat!
But you will not see the coach pass,
But you can hear its wheels
Go creak, creak, creaking by –
And a longing on you steals.
For you hear the Faeries laughing
In their weirdly shrill wild way;
And you wish that you could follow,
Or else that they would stay.
'Tis past – no one's returning –
You stand alone and still;
The sun is fast asleep now,
Beneath his quilt, the hill.

Stolen

Stolen from somebody's garden
As the day awoke in the East –
Stolen, a spray of wild white may
To deck the Faeries' feast.

Stolen from somebody's garden
As the day's hours journey along –
Stolen, a bundle of wild bluebells
To accompany the Faeries' song.

Stolen from somebody's garden
As the day went to sleep in the West –
Stolen, a handful of red rowan berries,
The fruit the Faeries like best.

Stolen from somebody's garden
When night took the place of day –
Stolen, a tiny dark-eyed child
Whom the Faeries found at play.

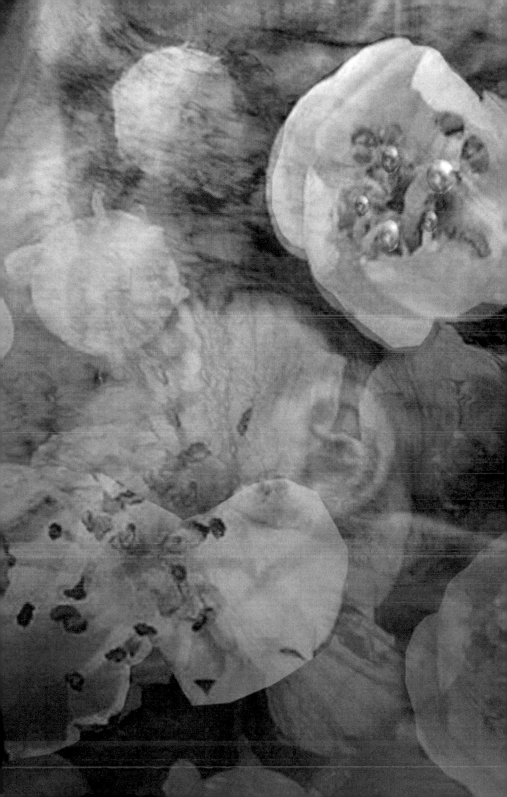

Wind Faeries

I can hear the Faeries of the wind
Laugh and whisper as they pass;
I can see clearly their wild brown locks
A-blowing when rustling through the grass.

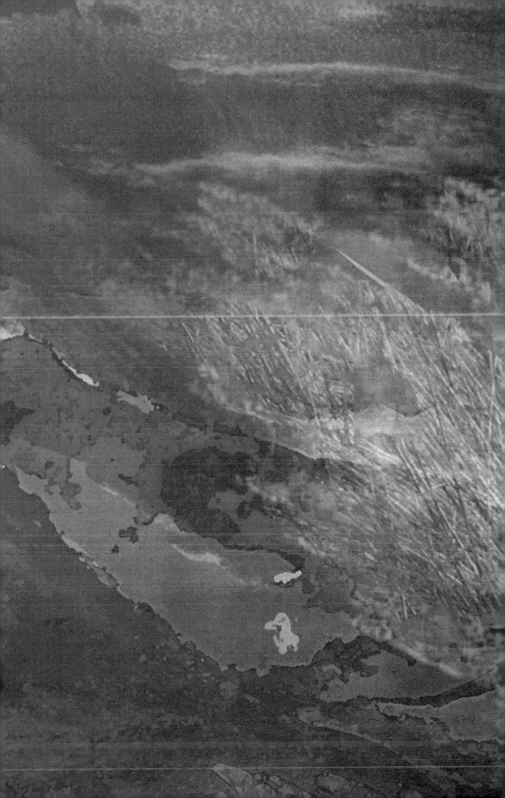

The Witch

The Witch with somebody dined that night,
  But she left her cat behind her;
And her friend, the owl, remarked with a scowl,
  "Twoo! She's left her luck behind her!"